FAMOUS AMERICANS IN HISTORY

Inventors & Inventions
2nd Grade U.S. History Vol 2

SPEEDY
PUBLISHING

Numerous American inventions have changed the world.

WILLIS CARRIER

was an American engineer, best known for inventing modern air conditioning. In 1915, he founded the Carrier Engineering Corporation.

BENJAMIN FRANKLIN

was one of the
Founding Fathers of
the United States. His
experiments with a kite
in a thunderstorm led
to the development of
the lightning rod.

JAMES NAISMITH

was a Canadian-American physical educator, physician, chaplain, sports coach and innovator. He invented the sport of basketball in 1891.

ALEXANDER GRAHAM BELL

though he was born in Scotland, Alexander Graham Bell didn't actually start inventing until he settled in Boston and became an American citizen. He invented the telephone.

CHARLES GOODYEAR

was an American self-taught chemist and manufacturing engineer who developed vulcanized rubber. He patented the process in 1844, licensed it to manufacturers and was ultimately hailed as a genius.

SAMUEL F. B. MORSE

was an American painter
and inventor. Morse
built the first American
telegraph around 1835.
Morse patented a working
telegraph machine in 1837.

THOMAS A. EDISON

was an American inventor.
He developed many
devices that greatly
influenced life around
the world, including
the phonograph.

ORVILLE & WILBUR WRIGHT

were two American brothers, inventors, and aviation pioneers. The first working airplane was invented, designed, made, and flown by the Wright brothers.

CYRUS MCCORMICK

was an American inventor. He developed the mechanical reaper. McCormick's invention automatically cut, threshed and bundled grain while being pulled through a field by horses.

Visit
BABY PROFESSOR
EDUCATION KIDS
www.BabyProfessorBooks.com
to download Free Baby Professor eBooks
and view our catalog of new and exciting
Children's Books